To my wife, Michelle, and my two daughters, Kayla and Hailey. I pray you always follow the Lord with your whole heart. Thank you for your love and support.

To my editor, my interior book designer, my illustrator, and my book cover designer. You helped bring this whole book to life.

Most importantly, this book is dedicated to God, my Lord and King. He brought together the team who worked on this project. He alone deserves all glory, honor and praise.

"So whether you eat or drink, or whatever you do, do it all for the glory of God."

1 Corinthians 10:31

Table of Contents

Ben caught himself fidgeting in his seat, nervously tapping his pencil against the palm of his hand. He was sitting in science class, just like he did every day, five days a week, one hundred eighty days out of the year. Science class was always his favorite class. He loved it! He hoped to be a scientist one day, discovering some neat new germ or figuring out a way to cure some disgusting disease. He always looked forward to learning about whatever lesson the teacher had planned.

Today was different though. Lately he had been struggling more with the things the teacher was teaching—well, ever since he had graduated to middle school actually. The lessons were beginning to get more confusing, and it frustrated him.

"I'm a good student," he muttered to himself. "I study hard. I get good grades. Why is this so hard all of a sudden?"

Today Mr. Stiller, his science teacher, was teaching the class something called "The Big Bang." The more the teacher talked, the more uneasy Ben felt.

This isn't what my mom and dad have taught me, Ben kept thinking. *Either my parents are right or Mr. Stiller is right. But how do I know who is telling me the truth?*

Mr. Stiller was saying that the universe was a big place, and was expanding or moving farther apart as time went by. *That must mean the universe used to be a whole lot smaller and more tightly packed together than it is today,* Ben mused, just as Mr. Stiller confirmed his thoughts.

"At some point in the distant past," Mr. Stiller explained, "the entire universe was crammed into a very small, very crowded space—say the size of a marble or even smaller." Ben didn't see how that could be possible.

In fact, he wasn't really sure it could be.

"Everything you can think of was there," Mr. Stiller continued. "Space, time, matter…"

"No way!" blurted Janine, Ben's friend who sat in the next row over.

"Yes, Janine… way!" Mr. Stiller laughed, "As I was saying, space, time, matter, energy, and all the physical laws of the universe, like gravity, began to exist at this point."

Okay, first we have nothing…then we have every-thing, Ben thought. Remembering what his parents had taught him about God, it all began to make sense.

God created it.

But Mr. Stiller wasn't done. And this was when Ben really began to have trouble with it all.

"The universe had a beginning," Mr. Stiller continued, bouncing on his toes. "Millions and billions and billions and millions of years ago, the universe exploded into existence on its own, with tremendous outward force. One day nothing…the next day, a universe." He smiled with satisfaction. "There are multiple scientific discoveries that confirm what we've come to call 'the Big Bang.'"

The bell rang and the kids all jumped from their seats. "Read pages 146 through 165 tonight! Pop quiz tomorrow!" Mr. Stiller yelled as everyone made a beeline for the door. Ben was too deep in thought to be in much of a hurry.

This Big Bang…what was it? Magic? How could nothing create everything? Ben was still troubled by the day's science lesson when he got to math class. He sat down at a desk away from everyone so he could think without being bothered.

Well, at least this is my last class of the day, he sighed. *Then I can go home and talk with my dad. This is all so confusing. If the Big Bang was the beginning, then what about God? Where does He come in?*

Ben's heart sank. *What if my parents are wrong and Mr. Stiller is right? What if there isn't a God?*

Ben wasn't hearing a word his math teacher was saying. When he was called to work a problem on the board, he got the answer wrong and the teacher chided him. "Get your head out of the clouds, Mr. Beckum. You've got a test this Friday, and you need to learn this stuff. If you get lost now, the rest of the year will not make any sense."

Ben scowled and returned to his seat. What did stupid math class matter if everything he believed turned out to be a lie? He was never so happy to hear the last bell of the day ring.

Ben's Big Bang Botheration

Ben didn't talk to his dad right away. To be honest, he was a little nervous. He didn't want to upset his dad or question his beliefs, but he needed some answers and he didn't know who else to go to. Drawing in a deep breath, he went to the study where his dad was working on some papers. His dad looked up and smiled when he saw Ben in the doorway. "Come on in, Son. Let me just get this one thing out of the way."

Ben shifted nervously as his dad finished some calculations, and then laid his pen down. He looked up at Ben with a slight frown. "What's on your mind? Sit down." Ben sat, and proceeded to tell his dad about science class that day and all the things Mr. Stiller had taught them. Ben's dad leaned forward, listening intently to Ben's story, and never said a word. Encouraged, Ben poured out his heart.

"Dad, where does God come in to all of this? Is Mr. Stiller right? Did everything just come from nothing? Is it possible that God doesn't exist?" Ben sat back, nervously anticipating his dad's response. There, he had said it. His doubts were out in the open.

His dad stood up. "Let's go for a drive, just you and me, and hash this out. We'll go get a Coke and head out to the park, how does that sound?"

It sounded great to Ben, who ran to get his jacket. Even though his questions hadn't been answered yet, he felt a sense of relief. His dad wasn't upset with him and he was willing to let Ben talk it out.

"First, Ben," his dad said as they headed down the road, "never be afraid to come to me or to God with your questions. I don't know everything, but between the two of us, we'll figure out the answers. And God is big enough to handle any of our doubts. He doesn't mind the questions either. In fact, He tells us to prove Him, to know that what He says is truth."

"Thanks, Dad," Ben said, relieved.

"There are three different belief systems that people have about the universe," his dad said as he parked the truck. They grabbed their Cokes and headed to a small table, away from the majority of the people there. "The first one is a belief that the universe always existed. Some religions even believe that God *is* the universe and that it has existed forever. This is called *pantheism* and there are a lot of people that think this way. The second one is that the universe popped into existence out of nothing, all by itself, like your teacher, Mr. Stiller, believes. This belief that nature is all there is, is called *naturalism* or *atheism*. And the third one is the belief that God created it all, like

you and I believe. And like you've come to see, not all these beliefs can be right."

"But how do we know what we believe is true?" Ben asked.

"Let's think about this a little bit further," Ben's dad replied. "Mr. Stiller is right about one thing—the universe did have a beginning. Not only has science proven this, but common sense does too. The universe cannot be without a beginning. All material things started at some point."

"Science and common sense agree that the universe is not infinitely old," his dad continued. "So those people who believe in a universe that has always been there, or that God is the physical stuff that makes up a universe that has always existed, are wrong. Can you see that? Are you comfortable with that reasoning?"

Ben nodded. "I'm with you so far."

"Now let's take Mr. Stiller's viewpoint that the universe just exploded out of nothing, all by itself. Have you known anything to just pop into existence all by itself?"

"No, but I'm only thirteen!" Ben laughed.

"Well, I'm a lot older than you," his dad grinned, "and I haven't seen anything like that either. In fact,

I don't know of anyone in all of history who has ever seen that happen. Look at a tree, a car, a house, a flower—anything at all…and you can see the truth of it. Everything that has a beginning had something that caused it to be."

"Yeah," Ben mused. "That makes sense."

"So, let's take that thought to its logical conclusion. If we agree that both scientific discovery and common sense tell us that the universe had a beginning…"

"…then it only makes sense that something caused that beginning!" Ben finished.

"Bingo," his dad replied.

"So you're saying Mr. Stiller is wrong then?"

"Yes, I am. Logic and reason tell us that something or someone had to have created the universe and started it in motion. So what would that something or someone have to be like?"

"Well, it would have to be really powerful and super smart," Ben offered.

"Agreed," said his dad. "It would also have to be timeless, since it was around before time began. And it couldn't take up space since there was no space before it was created, right?"

"Makes sense," Ben said.

"And it couldn't be made up of the physical stuff of the universe because none of that stuff existed before the universe was created."

Ben frowned in thought. "Yeah…"

"So let me ask you something. Who does that sound like to you?"

"It sounds like God."

"It sounds like God to me too," his dad agreed. "And this is

the God we read about every night in our Bibles."
He took a swallow of Coke. "Ben, God chose to
create everything out of nothing. He planned and

thought about everything, and then called it into
being. That He did this tells us that He's a personal
God, just like the God described in the Bible."

"Like it says in Genesis—He spoke and it was there!"

"Exactly. But what is even more personal is that God

didn't just speak man into existence, like He did everything else. He actually formed us Himself, out of the dust of the earth."

"I've never thought of that," Ben admitted. "But I do have one more question."

"Shoot."

"Well, what caused God?"

"Good question, Son. If you think back to what we've learned from the Bible, you'll remember that it says God is eternal, that He doesn't have a beginning and He has no end. You see, God created time when He created the universe. He's outside of time, unlike you and me or the rest of His creation. So if God doesn't have a beginning, He doesn't need a cause."

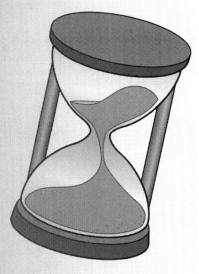

"Whoa, that's a lot to wrap my brain around," said Ben.

"Yeah, it is," his dad agreed.

"But I do feel a lot better after talking this out. Thanks, Dad."

"Not a problem," his dad said, ruffling his hair. "That's what dads are for. You need to know you can talk to me about anything. The door is always open, and I'll always be here when you need me."

Ben smiled at his dad, then gave him a big hug. "I know one thing," he said as they walked back to the car.

"What's that?" his dad asked.

"Tomorrow's science class will be a whole lot better than it was today!"

Ben's dad smiled as they made their way home.

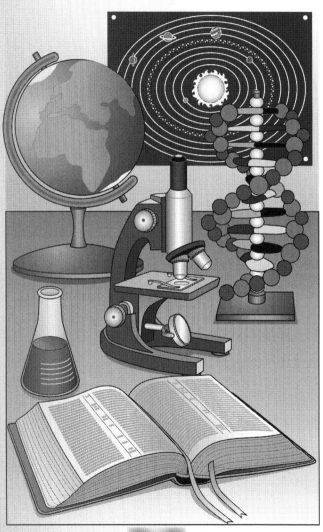

Important
Concepts
for Parents

Before beginning, I'd like to take a moment to discuss the word "tolerance" and ask you to consider what it means and what it does not mean. Tolerance is defined as, "remaining fair, objective, and permissive toward those whose opinions, practices, race, religion, nationality, etc. differ from one's own."[1] In regard to religion, tolerance does not mean to agree that all viewpoints are equal. This error in thinking leads to several erroneous assertions.[2] The first is called "religious pluralism," meaning no religion is exclusively true. The second is "multicultural diversity," or the belief that no truth transcends culture. Finally, it leads to "moral relativism," the belief that there are no moral values that are universal. These three assertions are false ways of looking at the world.

---

1 tolerance. Dictionary.com. Dictionary.com Unabridged. Random House, Inc. http://dictionary.reference.com/browse/tolerance (accessed: April 12, 2010).

2 M.J. Tyner, *Is Truth Relative or Objective?* (California: True-Way Tracts, 2009).

Truth is not always easy to hear, but claims of truth need to be examined and need to withstand such examination. This process is what determines truth from falsehood when analyzing any worldview. Each of the beliefs that are examined in this book cannot be equally true, as each one makes claims of truth that are contradictory to the others.

It is not my intent to prove that Christianity is true with 100% certainty. No worldview can do that. My intent is simply to demonstrate that Christianity offers the best explanation based on the evidence that is available to us all. The evidence for causation that is examined here is just one piece of a much larger puzzle, all of which points toward the truth of Christianity. We will examine additional pieces of the puzzle at a later time, as it's vital that our children are armed with the truth. They need to understand that their beliefs are anchored to it and that it's a truth that is knowable for all those who desire to seek it. Having said that, let's move on to the concepts discussed in this book.

There are three main viewpoints regarding the origin of the universe. The first viewpoint states the universe has always existed. This means that it's infinitely old. The second viewpoint says the universe popped into existence out of nothing. This means that it needs no explanation outside of itself, or put more simply, it created itself. The third viewpoint states that something created the universe. This means that a super-intelligent, super-powerful agent like God is required to logically explain all that we see. Only one of these viewpoints can be true. The evidence makes a compelling argument for the need of a creator.

Science and logic both point to a beginning of the universe. Scientifically, there is an abundant amount of evidence that suggests this. Logically, we know that time cannot be infinite.

Before we take a look at some of the reasons why we can know this, let's briefly consider this thing called the "Big Bang." There's a difference between the Big Bang (the idea that the universe somehow began to exist in a fiery explosion from a single point of nearly infinite density) and the belief that the universe created itself by popping into existence on its own, something we will discuss in greater detail later. It's important to understand that these are two very different concepts that are commonly lumped together and misunderstood.

The Big Bang and all of the evidence that supports it says nothing about how the universe was created or how it was set into motion. Where did all that matter and energy come from in the first place? What originally caused it to explode outward? The evidence remains silent about these questions and is only capable of proving that the universe had an absolute beginning, nothing more.

A closer look at some of the most significant evidence science uses to support the idea of this Big Bang, or beginning, brings us first to Einstein's theory of general relativity, postulated in the early 1900s. This theory predicted a beginning to the universe, which would later be supported by other discoveries. Einstein's theory (which has been verified meticulously) demanded an absolute beginning for

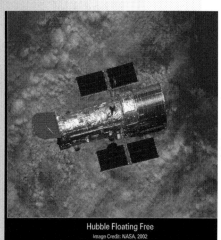

Hubble Floating Free
Image Credit: NASA, 2002

time, space, and matter, as well as demanding that they be co-relative (meaning that one could not exist without the others).[3]

In the 1920s, Edwin Hubble looked through his telescope and confirmed that the universe was indeed expanding from a

---

3 N.L. Geisler and F. Turek, *I Don't Have Enough Faith to be an Atheist* (Illinois: Crossway Books, 2004), 83-84.

single point just as Einstein had predicted. In the 1960s, Arno Penzias and Robert Wilson stumbled upon the cosmic background radiation (the afterglow from the fireball explosion that occurred in the beginning), again confirming previous predictions. Finally, in the 1990s, scientists found slight variations (ripples) in the temperature of the background radiation, yet again confirming previous predictions about this beginning.[4]

And there's more. Scientifically we know that time has a beginning—it is not infinite. Energy proves this point. The first law of

4 Geisler and Turek, 79-83.

thermodynamics states that the universe has a finite amount of energy. The second law of thermodynamics states, among other things, that the universe is running out of usable energy. The stars will one day burn themselves out. Since there is a finite amount of energy in the universe, and that energy is constantly being used up as time goes by, the universe could not have been around forever (or we would have run out of energy by now).[5]

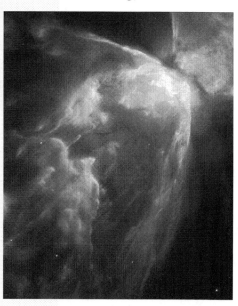

Photo of a dying star, courtesy of NASA, ESA and A. Zijlstra, UMIST, Manchester, UK

Also, through logical, deductive reasoning, we

---

5 Geisler and Turek, 76.

know that time is not infinite. History proves that yesterday had to occur before today could arrive. If yesterday had to occur before today could arrive, then the day before yesterday had to occur before it, and so on and so forth. There could not actually be an infinite number of days going back in time, because then the day you and I are living in right now would never exist. There has to be a first day in history in order for today to actually arrive in history.[6]

These facts are all important because each one supports an absolute beginning to our universe. They have effectively put an end to the idea that the universe is eternal, an idea held by many pantheistic religions and, as we shall see, most atheists before that time too.

What is pantheism? Pantheism is the general belief that the universe has always existed and that God *is* the physical "stuff" that makes up the universe. This means that God's essence of spirit is in the trees, the earth, the animals, etc. Many people still hold to

6 Geisler and Turek, 91.

this belief, but it simply cannot be confirmed by the reality in which we live. The universe has not always existed, and thus it requires an explanation outside of itself. Finite matter, or the physical "stuff" that makes up the universe, cannot be in turn made up of an infinite God.

What about the universe popping into existence by itself? Well, the universe could not have created itself, either. To highlight this point, it's important to understand a line of reasoning known as the Kalam cosmological argument. The argument consists of the following premises: [7]

1. Everything that has a beginning has something that caused it.

2. The universe had a beginning.

3. So, the universe had something that caused it.

Not one example of something popping into

---

7 J.P. Moreland & W.L. Craig, *Philosophical Foundations For A Christian Worldview* (Downers Grove: Intervarsity Press, 2003), 468.

33

existence, out of nothing and on its own, has ever been observed. On the other hand, a massive amount of observations over the course of human history tell us that the exact opposite is true. Things that have a beginning always have a cause.

Again, both scientific evidence and logic suggest that the universe had a beginning, so therefore it also had a cause. There is absolutely no good reason to believe that the universe created itself. None! The reason there's no good reason is because there's no evidence to support it. None!

This fact does not bode well for the naturalist, also known as an atheist. Naturalism, or atheism, is the general belief that nature is all that exists and thus, it needs no explanation beyond what nature can explain on its own. It's a belief that is consistent with the idea that the universe popped into existence by itself.

Since recent discoveries over the past one hundred years have put an end to the idea of an infinite universe (a view that most atheists adhered to previously), atheists have been forced to abandon their belief in an infinite universe and instead adhere to a new belief that the universe must have created itself. Unfortunately, this belief cannot be supported either through logic or science—concepts they profess to place a lot of faith in. Surprisingly, many people still hold to a belief that the universe popped into existence on its own, or created itself. Not only is this not true based on the evidence we have, it actually requires *more* faith to believe in than simply believing in God.

There is only one remaining explanation that adequately explains the evidence we have. The universe had a creator. An examination of the nature of that Creator is quite revealing. He must be intelligent, powerful, timeless, spaceless, and immaterial for sure. But mustn't He also be unique, uncaused, personal, creative, caring and omnipresent, just to name a few more qualities? [8]

It's not a coincidence that these attributes are very

8 Lee Strobel, *The Case for a Creator* (Grand Rapids, Michigan: Zondervan, 2004), 284-285

consistent with our God who is described on the pages in the book we call the Bible. His choice to create everything out of nothing (*ex nihilo*), just as the Bible claims, is also consistent with the most recent evidence and suggests that He is a personal God that is active in His creation (theism), not the type of God who has long since checked out and left us to fend for ourselves (deism). This attribute will be confirmed again and again by looking at additional evidences that will be examined in subsequent books.

It is at this point that some people may object, stopping to ask the following question: "Then what caused God?" There are a few things that need to be considered in relation to this question. The Kalam argument states that everything that has a beginning has something that caused it, not that everything has a cause. We know that the universe began to exist because God created it. God created time in the beginning of the universe along with everything else. He is not bound by the law of cause and effect (time) like the rest of His creation. The Bible teaches that God is eternal, meaning He has no beginning and He has no end. God did not have a beginning, so He does not need a cause. He is the uncaused cause, as He lies outside of His creation.

In conclusion, an honest examination of the evidence confirms that the biblical account of creation is true in regard to the beginning of the universe, an account which was written a mind-boggling 3,500 years ago or so. You can be confident in this fact. The scientific evidence supporting the biblical account that God created the universe out of nothing is stronger today than it has been at any other point in human history. Don't let anyone unwittingly convince you otherwise.

This series of books, as well as future series, published by Connect2Truth Books, are designed to be starting points, not ending points in your investigation of the Truth. Make the pursuit of Truth a priority! Continue your own personal investigation by visiting the websites listed in the "Additional Resources" section. Start reading and expanding your own understanding of these issues.

May God bless you and your family with a deeper, more personal faith in the process.

Today in Science Class

A Word from the Author

I hope you enjoyed reading this book as much as I enjoyed writing it. It is important to teach our children biblical truths. Truth is that which corresponds to reality, so it is important for them to understand that there are sound reasons for a belief in God, for a belief in the accuracy and trustworthiness of the Bible, and for a belief in Jesus Christ, our Lord and Savior.

Belief starts with the first five words of the Bible: "In the beginning God created...." These five words lay the foundation for a secure faith. If one truly believes these words, then nothing else in the Bible can really

become a barrier to belief. These five words will be the focus of the *Today in Science Class* series.

This claim that God created everything has

---

been under assault for many years. Evolution, eternal universes, and other explanations for how man and the universe came to exist attempt to remove God from the picture. Public education and our university campuses are teaching our children theories that are contradictory to a God-created universe. This series of books will address those theories.

The topic of the first book in the series, *Ben's Big Bang Botheration*, addresses causation. God is a necessary cause for the existence of our universe, a universe that has a beginning just as the Bible asserts. This is a powerful argument for the existence of God, and is supported both logically and scientifically. The evidence that supports it also happens to contradict all other worldviews except those that claim a personal God.

You might wonder why I've included what science has to say at all. To ignore what science has to say would be to ignore exactly what our children are being taught. I believe that this would be a mistake. I am not opposed to science; in fact, I believe that true science confirms God's existence.

In addition, I decided to remove the billions of years that are generally discussed with the Big Bang theory. I've done so to remove the familiar young earth vs. old earth debate, and instead, concentrate on the primary argument that our universe requires a creator.

I personally believe in the literal twenty-four-hour day account of creation, as I see no reason to doubt what the Bible clearly says. My God, who created the entire universe out of nothing, cannot be put into a box. He is not bound by His creation to do things in any particular way in which we think He should do them. He can do

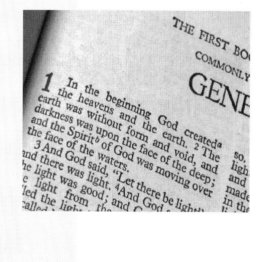

anything He chooses to do, in any way He chooses to do it.

My belief in God does not hinge on whether or not the latest evidence supports a young earth or old earth, nor does my belief hinge on whether or not the Big Bang theory is true, as there are other evidences that confirm a beginning. My faith hinges on the fact that I know, "In the beginning God created…." That's all I need to know for sure. All other arguments may be worth arguing over, but they are secondary arguments to me.

This book was designed to be a tool for you to use in your quest to arm your children with the Truth. It was designed to educate both you and your children in some basic apologetics, and to allow you the opportunity to have meaningful conversions about the things of God. Due to the limits of this book's format, everything could not possibly be explained in detail. My intent is for you to enrich this book with both Scripture and conversation.

May God bless you in your effort to do so.

Today in Science Class

Additional
Resources

If you found value in this book's message, then please help spread the word by telling a friend about this website:

www.TodayInScienceClass.com

For additional Christian resources, please visit this website:

www.Connect2Truth.com

Connect2**Truth**
BOOKS

We would love to hear from you. Please send your comments about this book to:

reviews@Connect2Truth.com

Thank you!

Made in the USA
Charleston, SC
27 July 2010